Exploring Our Rainforest

RETICULATED PYTHON

TAMRA B. ORR

CHERRY LAKE Publishing

Published in the United States of America by Cherry Lake Publishing
Ann Arbor, Michigan
www.cherrylakepublishing.com

Content Adviser: Dr. Stephen S. Ditchkoff, Professor of Wildlife Ecology, Auburn University, Alabama
Reading Adviser: Marla Conn, ReadAbility, Inc.

Photo Credits: ©Wannachatp/Dreamstime.com, cover, 1, 9; ©Stef Bennett/Dreamstime.com, 5; ©Accipiter/www.
wikimedia.org/CC-BY-SA 2.0, 6; ©feathercollector/Shutterstock Images, 7; ©Lukas Blazek/Dreamstime.com, 11;
©Brian Cressman, 12; ©cowboy5437/Thinkstock, 13; ©Thammanoon Panyakham/Dreamstime.com, 15; ©Dorling
Kindersley/Thinkstock, 17; ©fivespots/Shutterstock Images, 19; ©RainForest Adventures, 21; ©worananphoto/
Shutterstock Images, 22; ©feather0510/depositphotos, 25; ©Melinda Millward, 26; ©Lisette van der Hoorn/
Shutterstock Images, 27; ©Leah Marshall/Thinkstock, 29

Library of Congress Cataloging-in-Publication Data

Orr, Tamra, author.
Reticulated python / Tamra B. Orr.
    pages cm. — (Exploring our rainforests)
    Summary: "Introduces facts about reticulated pythons, including physical features, habitat, life cycle, food, and threats
to these rainforest creatures. Photos, captions, and keywords supplement the narrative of this informational text."
— Provided by publisher.
    Audience: Ages 8-12.
    Audience: Grades 4 to 6.
    Includes bibliographical references and index.
    ISBN 978-1-63188-979-0 (hardcover) — ISBN 978-1-63362-018-6 (pbk.) — ISBN 978-1-63362-057-5 (pdf) —
ISBN 978-1-63362-096-4 (ebook) 1. Reticulated python—Juvenile literature. I. Title.

    QL666.O63O77 2015
    597.96'78—dc23   2014024968

Cherry Lake Publishing would like to acknowledge the work of
The Partnership for 21st Century Skills. Please visit www.p21.org
for more information.

Printed in the United States of America
Corporate Graphics

ABOUT THE AUTHOR

Tamra Orr is a full-time writer and author living in the gorgeous Pacific Northwest. She loves her job because she learns more about the world every single day and then turns that information into pop quizzes for her patient and tolerant children (ages 23, 21, and 18). She has written more than 350 nonfiction books for people of all ages, so she never runs out of material and is sure she'd be a champion on Jeopardy!

TABLE OF CONTENTS

HIDING IN THE BRANCHES

The young reticulated python coils itself around the tree branch and continues waiting for its meal to come along. The python is very still and patient. It can wait for hours, even days. The rainforest grows darker and darker. While many animals are preparing to sleep for the night, others, like the python, are awake and ready to hunt.

There is a soft rustle in the grass below. Is it danger, or is it dinner? The python's tongue flicks in and out, trying to catch the scent of the animal in the air. Small

Pythons must be alert when hunting.

RANGE MAP

- ARCTIC OCEAN
- North America
- ATLANTIC OCEAN
- PACIFIC OCEAN
- South America
- Europe
- Asia
- Africa
- INDIAN OCEAN
- PACIFIC OCEAN
- Australia

RANGE OF RETICULATED PYTHON

Reticulated pythons live in Southeast Asia.

The python uses its tongue to sense where other animals are.

pits above its mouth tell it that the nearby creature is not a threat. The meal waiting below is a baby bearded pig. With its bristly coat, wiry beard, and long nose, the pig is searching for a tasty earthworm or piece of fruit hidden in the leaves on the forest floor. It's too busy to notice the threat just a few inches above its head.

Slowly, sneakily, the reticulated python lowers itself toward its prey. The baby pig interrupts its hunting and looks back over its hairy shoulder. The snake is wrapping itself around the pig's neck, and now it sinks its sharp teeth into the animal's skin. The python squeezes the pig's body tighter and tighter.

Minutes later, the python's jaw stretches out almost impossibly wide in order to fit the bearded pig into its mouth. The pig is a huge dinner for the young python, which won't have to hunt again for weeks. The snake's patience has paid off.

GO DEEPER

THE RETICULATED PYTHON IS KNOWN AS AN AMBUSH PREDATOR. WHAT DO YOU THINK THIS TERM MEANS?

The python has sharp teeth, but it relies on the strength of its muscles to kill its prey.

Nature's Pattern

Reticulated pythons would be champions at playing hide and seek. Not only can they pick a spot and stay there for hours without moving, but they are also wearing the perfect disguise. The python's skin is decorated in a pattern of gray and light brown, with markings in green, yellow, gold, and black. This pattern gave the pythons the name *reticulated*. The word means "markings like a pattern of lines or a net." This uneven pattern is known in nature as **disruptive** coloration. It is a very effective type of **camouflage**. A python on the ground is almost impossible to see amid the mud, leaves, and plants.

The skin of a reticulated python has a recognizable pattern.

BODY DIAGRAM

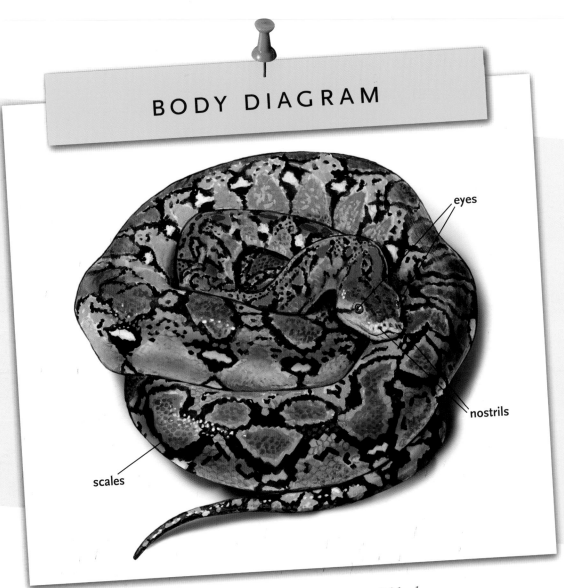

eyes

nostrils

scales

The reticulated python has a long, powerful body.

[21ST CENTURY SKILLS LIBRARY]

Pythons are able to curl up in small spaces.

The colors and patterns on the snake's skin blend in perfectly with their surroundings. These pythons are found throughout parts of Southeast Asia, including the rainforests of Vietnam, Malaysia, Indonesia, the Philippines, and on various islands such as Borneo and Sumatra. Their camouflage makes it possible for pythons to hang in trees, slither on the ground, and swim in rivers, lakes, and ponds without being seen. Most animals never see these snakes coming, which is remarkable considering the python's size!

The average python can grow to 15 or 20 feet (4.5 or 6.1 meters) long. That is almost as long as a minivan. Many pythons, however, grow much, much larger. They can grow to 30 feet (9.1 m) long, which is the length of two minivans put together. The longest reticulated python ever found was in 1991 and was listed in *The Guinness Book of World Records* that year. That python measured 32 feet 9 ½ inches (10 m)! These snakes weigh hundreds of pounds and get as big as 12 inches (30.5 centimeters) in **diameter**.

What makes these pythons so dangerous? They have two amazing secret weapons.

A python's body is the thickest right after it has finished a meal.

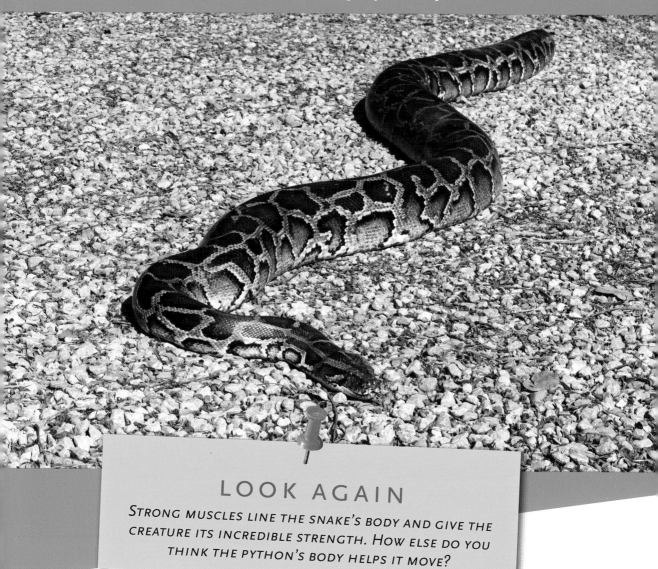

LOOK AGAIN

STRONG MUSCLES LINE THE SNAKE'S BODY AND GIVE THE CREATURE ITS INCREDIBLE STRENGTH. HOW ELSE DO YOU THINK THE PYTHON'S BODY HELPS IT MOVE?

Jaws and Muscles

In addition to being extremely large, reticulated pythons are unique in several ways. When this snake kills an animal, it does not rip it into parts. Instead, the python swallows its meal whole! Consider that its diet may include deer, pigs, antelope, rats, monkeys, sheep, leopards, and even porcupines. Some of these animals are quite large! So how can the snake swallow them whole?

The python's first secret weapon is its jaw. The jaw is made of four moveable parts. These parts are connected by very stretchy **ligaments** that allow the jaw to open

A reticulated python strangles its prey before swallowing it whole.

even wider than a right angle. That would be like a human being eating an entire cantaloupe in a single bite. Along with that **flexible** jaw, the snake has two rows of very sharp, backward-curving teeth that work like sharp hooks. Given all this equipment, it is not surprising that any animal caught by a reticulated python is not able to get away.

In addition to its amazingly flexible jaws, the python has a second secret weapon—its muscles. The python's body is lined with powerful muscles. Once the python has its prey, it wraps its long body around it and squeezes tighter and tighter. It is a truly **lethal** squeeze.

Soon the animal can no longer breathe, and it **suffocates**. The python knows it's time to let go when it can no longer feel the creature's heart beating. At last, the time has come to swallow and **digest**—a process that may take weeks to months!

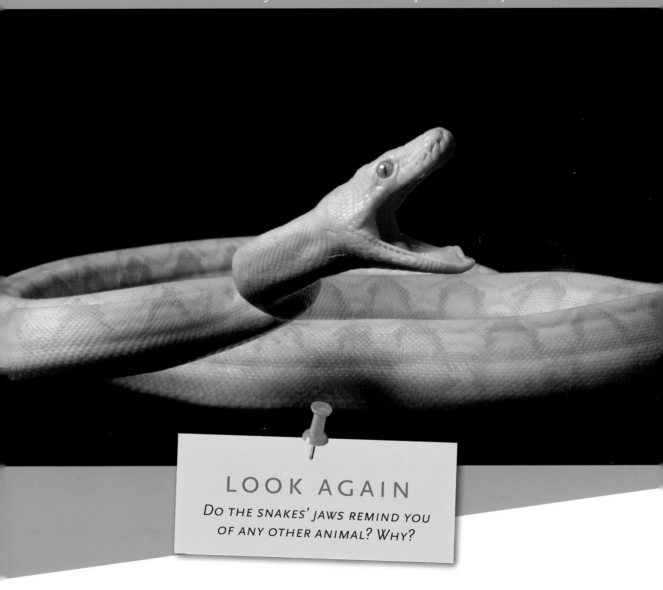

This albino reticulated python is missing the familiar colors that the species normally has.

LOOK AGAIN

DO THE SNAKES' JAWS REMIND YOU OF ANY OTHER ANIMAL? WHY?

BORN READY

It is hard to believe that the huge reticulated python could have anything in common with a farm chicken, but it does. Like chickens, these snakes lay eggs, and they work to keep those eggs warm until they are ready to hatch.

Most boa constrictor-type snakes bear live young, but reticulated pythons lay between 25 and 100 eggs at a time. Once laid, the eggs are kept warm by the mother snake coiling around them and vibrating to raise the temperature. The eggs are white and about the same size as a chicken egg. The shells, however, are not hard. Instead, they are soft and leather-like. While the babies are **incubating**, the female snake wraps around the eggs to keep them warm. She does this for around 3 months. If the temperature drops below 89 degrees Fahrenheit

A mother python guards her eggs.

Crocodiles are one animal that pythons need to watch out for.

(31.6 degrees Celsius), the snake uses its muscles for something entirely different. It vibrates, much like people do when they shiver. This helps to raise the temperature next to the eggs.

When it is time for the baby pythons to hatch, their mothers are already gone. From the beginning, these **hatchlings** are on their own. Hatching begins when the baby snake uses a sharp tooth to tear a hole in the eggshell. Once the hole is big enough, the snake slides out. It is already 2 to 3 feet (61 to 91 cm) long, and it is born already knowing how to hunt.

Hatchlings have to be careful because, while they are hunting for food, other animals are hunting for them! Hawks, cobras, and crocodiles consider these little pythons a tasty treat. Two weeks after they are born, the hatchlings shed their skin. This process may sound strange, but it is similar to a person taking off a pair of socks at night. Shedding its skin does not hurt the snake, and it allows the snake to keep growing. Pythons live as long as 15 years in the wild or 25 years in **captivity**.

THINK ABOUT IT

WHY ARE THE BABY SNAKES BORN ALREADY ABLE TO HUNT AND LIVE ON THEIR OWN? HOW CAN THEY SURVIVE WITHOUT THEIR PARENTS TO HELP RAISE THEM?

CHAPTER 5

FROM BRANCHES TO BOOTS

Looking at a huge reticulated python, it is hard to imagine anything threatening it. What could possibly stop a snake this long, strong, and powerful? Most of the time, nothing. But there are times when pythons are **vulnerable**.

Adult pythons are sometimes in danger while they are eating or when they have just finished eating a very large prey. While swallowing a large animal, pythons cannot defend themselves. After eating, they cannot move quickly. At such times, the snake can become a

Pythons are vulnerable after eating huge meals.

Pythons are sometimes able to escape other animals, but humans still create problems for them.

nice snack for big cats like lions and leopards and birds of prey such as hawks and eagles.

The most serious threat to reticulated pythons, however, is humans. The rainforests where these snakes live are constantly being damaged by logging and mining projects. The other human threat comes from a completely different place—the world of fashion.

Every year, thousands of reticulated pythons are killed simply for their skin. Snakes have beautiful patterns that help protect and hide them in the wild.

Cutting down trees forces pythons to find shelter somewhere else.

Unfortunately, those patterns are also what many people want on their handbags, belts, watchbands, vests, wallets, briefcases, and boots. Millions of dollars are spent every year throughout the world for these products.

Other pythons are captured and sold to zoos or pet stores. Circuses often include these huge snakes in their shows. While many zookeepers, pet owners, and circus performers treat their snakes with care and kindness, many do not. Then these huge snakes suffer.

Reticulated pythons are stunningly beautiful creatures that slither, crawl, swim, and squeeze. Reticulated pythons are one reason the world's rainforests are such fascinating and exotic places.

Some people think snakeskin looks very fashionable.

LOOK AGAIN

WHAT IS IT ABOUT SNAKESKIN PRODUCTS THAT APPEALS TO PEOPLE?
WHERE DO YOU THINK MOST OF THEM ARE SOLD?

THINK ABOUT IT

- In chapter 2, you learned that reticulated pythons have "disruptive coloration" to help disguise them in the rainforest. What other animals can you think of that use this method of staying safe?

- Do you think there should be laws put in place about selling real snakeskin products? What rules would you suggest?

- Why would reticulated pythons be especially slow moving after eating a large meal?

- How could a python be a threat to human beings? Why is it so dangerous to have a python as a pet?

LEARN MORE

FURTHER READING

Arlon, Penelope. *Reptiles*. New York: Scholastic, 2013.

Bishop, Nic. *Snakes*. New York: Scholastic, 2012.

Editors of Time for Kids with Lisa Jo Rudy. *Snakes!* New York: HarperCollins Publishers, 2005.

Goldish, Meish. *Reticulated Python: The World's Longest Snake*. New York: Bearport Publishing, 2010.

WEB SITES

The Animal Spot—Reticulated Python
www.theanimalspot.com/reticulatedpython.htm
Read about the location, habitat, diet, size, and description of these amazing pythons.

Big Animals—The Reticulated Python
www.big-animals.com/the-reticulated-python/
Read about the python at this site, which features the biggest, longest, heaviest, and tallest animals in the world.

Rainforest Animals—Reticulated Python
www.rainforestanimals.net/rainforestanimal/reticulatedpython.html
Find out which animals share the rainforest environment with the reticulated pythons.

GLOSSARY

camouflage (KAM-uh-flahzh) a skin pattern that alters an animal's appearance, making it harder to be seen

captivity (kap-TIV-i-tee) the state of being held, as in a zoo

diameter (dye-AM-ih-tur) a straight line through the center of a circle connecting opposite sides

digest (di-JEST) to break down food in the digestive system

disruptive (dis-RUHP-tiv) disturbing or interrupting something that is happening

flexible (FLEK-suh-buhl) able to bend or stretch without breaking

hatchlings (HACH-lingz) young reptiles recently out of their eggs

incubating (ING-kyuh-bate-ing) sitting on or keeping eggs warm until they hatch

lethal (LEE-thuhl) deadly or fatal

ligaments (LIG-uh-munts) stretchy tissues that connect muscles to bones

suffocates (SUHF-uh-kates) dies after being prevented from taking a breath

vulnerable (VUHL-nur-uh-buhl) capable of being wounded or hurt

INDEX